AMERICAN YARD

AMERICAN YARD

POEMS BY DOLORES HAYDEN

Dolores Hayden

David Robert Books

Published by David Robert Books
P.O. Box 541106
Cincinnati, OH 45254-1106

ISBN: 1932339418
LCCN: 2003116002

Design: Amanda Bowers
Typeset in Adobe Jenson
Cover: Alexander Jackson Davis, "American Cottage No. 1" from
Rural Residences, 1837. Courtesy of the Beinecke Rare Book and Manuscript
Library, Yale University.
Author Photograph: © Michael Marsland

Poetry Editor: Kevin Walzer
Business Editor: Lori Jareo

Visit us on the web at www.davidrobertbooks.com

For Laura Hayden Marris

YARD

OE: *geard*, fence, dwelling, house, region.

OS: *gard*, enclosure, field, dwelling, garden.

OHG: *gart*, circle, ring. ON: *garth*, yard, farm.

Noun: fence, field, enclosure, dwelling, region; symbol of authority; unit of measure; by the yard (at great length); yard of land (thirty acres).

Verb, tr.: to enclose, to store up, to herd.

Slang: the virile member; yard of ale (tall glass of ale); yard of satin (glass of gin); yard of tin (coachman's horn); hundred dollar bill; go the whole nine yards, go to extremes.

ACKNOWLEDGMENTS

I would like to thank the editors of many journals for first publication of the poems in this collection:

Able Muse, "Language of the Flowers," "Farandole," "Facts of Life," "Local Knowledge"

Crab Orchard Review, "The Milliner's Proposals"

Electrum, "Revenge with Ice Palace"

The Formalist, "Pregnant in June"

Hellas, "Private Geography," "Language of the Fan," "On E-mail"

Landscape Journal, "Invitation to Mr. John Brinckerhoff Jackson"

The Kenyon Review, "Target Practice"

Manhattan Poetry Review, "Yesterday I Learned the Earth Is Flat"

Michigan Quarterly Review, "Taxidermy"

Poetry Northwest, "Pickers' Market"

Poets On, "Connoisseur"

Salt (U.K.), "Sapphics for Saint Ursula"

Slate, "Pacific Airstream Reaches New England"

Southwest Review, "For Rent"

Verse Daily, "For Rent," "Pacific Airstream Reaches New England," "Pregnant in June," "Target Practice"

The Yale Review, "Cadillac Ranch," "On the Hundred-Percent Corner"

Poems which appear in anthologies include:

City A/Z, eds. Steve Pile and Nigel Thrift, "Lunch With Giambattista
     Nolli," "Taxidermy," "On the Fault Line"

Imagining the City, ed. Setha Low, "Lunch with Giambattista Nolli"

Margin: Songs Sung in Island Time, "Target Practice"

Motherhood and Space, eds. Caroline Wiedmer and Sarah Hardy, "Station
Zero"

"Language of the Flowers" won the Poetry Society of America's *The Writer
     Magazine*/Emily Dickinson Award.

"Pickers' Market" was runner-up for the Poetry Society of America's Robert
     Winner Award.

"Language of the Fan" won the *Hellas* Award.

I am especially greatful to Robert L. Barth who published two chapbooks
from this collection, *Playing House* (Edgewood, KY: R.L.B., 1998) and *Line
Dance* (Edgewood, KY: R.L.B., 2001).

CONTENTS

I.

II.

III.

III.

I.

JULY

We lie on a fieldstone bridge across the creek,
absorb its stored-up noonday heat.
A garter snake lives under the ledge,
with one small shrug shines yellow-banded,
a perfect skin of empty stripes
left in the grass beside our feet.
I'd like to learn to shed.

We stretch in the meadow, fireflies lift above
the hill's seductive curve, a hiplike
shape I've never quite deciphered.
Alight they mount past oaks' dark crowns,
extend the handle of the Plough,
tweak the Serpent's tail, fill
the whole of Cornwall Hollow.

Wonder enters, gravid as desire,
the weight of what we know, or don't—
zoology, astronomy,
cold light in fireflies' blinking tails,
the warmth of Venus miles away.
Just like the wingless females, mute,
we're grounded for display,

attached to earth revolving a thousand miles
an hour. Sky-houses crowd our charts,
no city lights can reach us spinning.
We never say July can't last,
we shrug and shed. Male thousands pulse
cold signal lights like far, hot stars,
we fuse, we are so near.

FOR RENT

Difficile est proprie communia dicere.
It is difficult to speak of what is common in a way of your own.
—Horace, *Ars Poetica*

I.

In a sheath of weathered boards, false front
on all four sides, the red house rides
a saddle of eroded ground

and leans as if it might wash down
in winter rains. But reader, here
you see the oldest house around.

It's much too high for neighborhood.
From worn-out steps long views expand,
command wide axes everywhere,

entice your kind of hairpin vision,
a swaying wide and cambering in.
The city sounds don't reach us here.

2.

Hummingbirds sip hibiscus cups.
A red-tailed hawk circles, plummets
into the canyon, reappears.

The mailbox sags. Century plants
split broken, almost impassable steps—
and flower every hundred years.

Yes, you know the place needs work,
ungrudging cultivation, a poet
like you to weed in noonday heat,

count pairs of small blue butterflies,
repair the broken hearth, stoke fires
with eucalyptus or mesquite.

3.

Due north lie wooded peaks too steep
for cut and fill. Packs of coyotes
scavenge their slopes, sing through the nights.

Eastward sits gated Mount Olympus,
muscle-bound mansions, turquoise pools,
an acre Omega, party lights.

If you stare south across the grid
where cowboy towns crowd French chateaux,
terrazzo stars spell HOLLYWOOD.

Look west, you'll glimpse Pacific swells
beyond the park where hungry men
cut whirligig toys they trade for food.

4.

The old red house rents month-to-month,
no boiler plate, security,
sometimes, late summer, the well goes dry.

You think you might be interested?
Skywriting pilots buzz this house,
roaring cloud vowels a half-mile high.

Dusk swims with wispy backlit cirrus,
three-mile nouns stretch out your eye,
wild verbs advance, alacrify,

moonrise carves commas in your sky.
So, you're sure you want to sign?
Hooked on the place? So am I.

INVITATION TO
MR. JOHN BRINCKERHOFF JACKSON

(after Elizabeth Bishop and Pablo Neruda)

From Santa Fe, over Route 66, on this dry morning,
  do come riding.
With a trail of motorcycle exhaust,
  do come riding
past the calm facades of ordinary white houses
streaming out of a desert sky
over the shining amusement park of strip construction,
  do come riding.

On the used car lots, pennants and tinsel are flapping. Truckers
converse, hundreds of brake lights
blink and CB radios play all over the West.
Behold: Interstate highways engineered
to deliver countless miles for gasoline taxes,
Truck City in lieu of silver spoons.
The ride is safe, we expect no smoggy weather.
The roads unroll like an essayist's lead this morning.
  Do come riding.

Come with the silver spurs of each cowboy boot
inset with a turquoise star,
with a motorcycle helmet full of antique road signs,
with who knows how many cultural geographers clinging
to the back of your black leather jacket,
    do come riding.

Bearing an invisible perspective camera,
a small aristocratic twinkle and six wild flowers,
    do come riding.
Yards and mini-malls soak up the sun: Los Angeles
buzzes with speculators this fine evening,
      please come riding.

Speeding past billboards advertising unspoiled landscapes,
past the wrecked-car yards and the x-rated movies,
the topless bars and the toxic incinerators,
when condos assault your goggled eyes
you can see through them
an orderly landscape gridded for pioneers,
    do come riding.

For you the design school professors smile
like the parents of debutantes with unfilled dance cards,
for you the corporate architects lie in wait
in fluorescent-lit drafting rooms,
ready to mount and ride through the night
out into your secret America,
    do come riding.

We can eat Franco-Japanese food, we can go swimming,
or critique the movie stars' houses
with our old-fashioned architectural prejudices,
or we can ignore it all, but please,
    do come riding.

With the mandarins of architectural history
mumbling about classical orders around you,
with humor that sets your eyes alight
like headlamps shining,
    do come riding.

Drive like a semi on a freeway,

drive like a vacationer on a minor road,

with a long discursive talk about space,

from Santa Fe, over Route 66, on this fine morning,

    do come riding.

PICKERS' MARKET

Brimfield, Massachusetts

I sell my shawl,   cerise silk,
to a made-up man   in a maroon Mercedes.
$16.70.   No sales tax.
My partner nabs   a Navy man's ribbons,
Purple Hearts   and Pacific pins
with Silver Stars,   sweeping away
his whole war   for a wrinkled bill.
Bartering, I bully   someone into buying
a pig long-parted   from a park carousel,
with hot-pink haunches   and heliotrope hooves.
It stands unsteadily   by a sagging pie safe
with scattered stars   in a tin sky.
I tell tales   of tourist potential,
rarities, restorations,   like the rural wife
who drilled the stars   to distract from dozens
of leathery pies.   A New Londoner likes
our tiger-maple table   with the tipping top.
It looks legitimate,   we unload it.
I polish a pair   of pewter giraffes,
trade these twins   to a Toronto collector
for a battered boat   with a broken bowsprit.

We need and know   nothing but prices.

Did I ever wish   for this wandering life?

As he ties the twine   on our torn tarpaulin,

sun ruddles   the schooner's sails,

summons several   small seas

an earnest boy   easily exhausted.

He dreamed all day   of wider waters.

I climb in the Chevy.   He chooses our road.

WIDOW SEWING WORK CLOTHES QUILTS, GEE'S BEND, ALABAMA

*Women who could not afford blankets made quilts;
women who could not afford cloth used old work clothes.*

She cuts his shirts and jeans and overalls,
piecing the quilts to keep six children warm
as early winter needles through log walls.

Late fall, frost rims the creek. The weather stalls.
Her husband's dead—took chill after a storm.
She grasps his shirts and jeans and overalls,

unstitches pockets, rips his 40 talls
with knees knocked-out from plowing round the farm.
As early winter needles through log walls,

she saves the chest and shoulders, strips all
sound cloth from thigh and seat, takes out an arm.
She clasps his shirts and jeans and overalls—

beneath the pockets, some fresh denim falls
inside a faded field. She's strapped, needs swarm.
As early winter needles through log walls,

old sun-struck cloth wraps babies like fine shawls,
embraces them with shapes a man's limbs form.
She holds his shirts and jeans and overalls
as early winter needles through log walls.

LOCAL KNOWLEDGE

Sap moon, grass moon, milk moon, rose moon—
from March to June, the almanac
weds farms to skies. I'm new in Maine.

July—two soda fountain stools,
green orbs of leatherette and chrome,
swing round, he talks of molecules

and stars. Come hay moon songs pulse from
the neon jukebox, planets pattern
everything from shirts to gum.

By August zany drive-in plots
mix up the spheres. Space aliens
make love and war, earth astronauts

blast laser guns at my tanned feet
extended toward a corn moon sky
above his borrowed car's back seat.

Fruit moon: I never figure out
when he decides we're through. I pack
for school, I ask around about

his newest flame. The hunter's moon,
the beaver moon, they're all the same
to me, until one afternoon,

below a crescent on the wane,
I recognize hay moons, corn moons
still shine on him in Deer Isle, Maine,

and all the everyday things worn
and sung and touched and heard and seen.
He can't recall the summer that I mean.

SECOND MARRIAGE

Week after week in early fall we hike
the wasted trail along the dry creek bed,
through withered grasses, past charred laurel groves
where every living thing has weathered fire.
No bloom survives on any sooty stalk.
We climb. Packs chafe our shoulders' fragile flesh.
We find no new green laurel, so we talk
of sound succession, taking our weekly walks
until pale leaves uncurl beside burned stumps
from seeds that sprouted in the heart of fire.
Wild paintbrush pierces blackened slopes, and shoot
by shoot embraces dry Topanga earth,
kindles the wild new place paired souls can claim,
the canyon floor of flowering inch-high flame.

LANGUAGE OF THE FLOWERS

The career of flowers differs from ours only in audibleness. —Emily Dickinson

Affection jonquils can bespeak,
red tulips, Love. Strategic, meek,

she shears some lilies for her carafe,
adds jasmine sprays to telegraph

hesitant Sensuality,
plan pleasures neighbors need not see.

A full-blown rose, Meet Me Tonight,
placed over two buds, warns Secret Flight.

Lush honeysuckle may confuse,
since Bonds of Love might still refuse

if she's twined sprigs of dark green holly,
Foresight, with columbine for Folly.

And if some love has proven false,
fallen for one of her friends, or worse...

it's lobelia, Malevolence,
dark-stemmed blue buds, small ones. She's tense,

troubled, teary with dismay.
She adds no card to this bouquet,

dead leaves spell Melancholy, season
favors sour whortleberry, Treason.

PACIFIC AIRSTREAM REACHES NEW ENGLAND

86 degrees, December

Balmy high. The New Dawns start in June—
eight Decembers have I lived here, never
smelled pink bushes in the winter. Ever.
Sun-warmed, thawed, and lazy, I won't prune.
Basking, I forget it's almost Christmas,
shed my heavy sweater. Grass needs mowing,
weighted with full blossoms canes keep growing.
Short-tailed starlings swarm our narrow isthmus,
crowd the maples, cackle ordinary
happiness, black iridescence, hot noon.
Listen: soot wings wheeling snap warm air.
Roses bud to open. Don't be wary.
Weather beggars winter. Love now, not soon.
Yes, we'll stretch out on the beach. I dare.

HUSBAND AND WIFE WITH SNOWY EGRETS

Mid-afternoon, we slip in
at the top of the tide. Silent
creatures of the air,

we slide down the grass bank
without a splash, divide
slick mud and mussels,

startle shifts of minnows.
Backstroking toward the bay,
suspended in salt water,

we breathe spartina, samphire.
Fawns nibble the far shore.
Egrets shuffle in the shallows,

stab their black and yellow bills
like sharp pencils.
We don't distract them

or the osprey overhead
who claws a snapper blue.
Stalkers of sidewalks, cousins

to cars, we're weightless when
we frog-kick, breast-stroke, wallow
in late September's warmth

until we haul ourselves back
over a crumbling shelf
of fiddler crabs and oyster shells.

Behind the egrets, up the creek,
a shingled boathouse rides,
its wide, white-framed door

a sign of summers past crossed
in weathered wood, square
divided foursquare.

REVENGE WITH ICE PALACE

Winter seized last week's
rough water, halted our river.
Night after night, alone,
sleeping uneasily,
I build in old St. Paul.

It's time to harvest ice:
yard after yard, my bevel
rasps and groans as I scrape
the surface, plane it down.
Hissing, my marker grids

the cubic cold I prod
with pointed iron tongs.
Ice upon ice, here's mortar
to set the stone. These walls
won't fail me, they will hold you

if I can't. Buttresses fly,
I brace the tower, top it
with your chill room. Short sunsets
gild the west façade,
after it's dark, I light

the new electric current,
make ice walls blush light pink,
brumid salons look warm.
Free-skating couples pause
to toast each other, sip

champagne. The public revels
won't include you, Lover.
You'll miss the waltz, when couples
kiss as Roman Candles
whiz, pierce Old Man Winter,

beckon to Spring. An empress
once commanded her man
an ice bed with a snow quilt.
You might survive a week
in the ice palace. (He did.)

But in my cold dreams you don't.

HOSPICE

Death squeezes in the crowded elevator,
presses "Door Close," starts intravenous music.
When we both get off, she strides ahead of me,

humming, nodding at prints on Third Floor West—
an empty Adirondack chair, an oak
stripped bare, glass gripped in tight aluminum frames.

In the waiting room she straddles a plastic bench,
winks, lights up while nurses hiss, "No Smoking!"
Over my shoulder she absorbs the headlines,

"Kosovo Strafed," "Himalayan Border Strife,"
"A Midnight Race on Interstate Kills Three,"
"New Baby Drowned in Baptism Rites." She grins.

We browse the gift shop, helium balloons
float "Hang in There!" "Get Well Soon!" and "Love."
She sneaks a look at me, she shakes her head,

picks up a pocket comb to wheeze kazoo
off-key, her weary tune winds and wanders
and almost weeps—but—she wants a change.

In the bar across the street, her hand's a winner
at doomsday stud, she sweeps the pot, buys rounds
for young mechanics on break-time from the airport.

She taunts two girls to try exotic smokes,
dares older guys to drag their cars down Main
when all the bars have finally closed. She's bored,

she's coming back to stalk the low-e windows,
to shut white blinds fixed fast behind the glass
inside my mother's room. She stops, confides,

"I'm out of work right now. But not for long.
This is my floor, the hospice for the dying—
your mother, here, looks like a saint to me."

TAXIDERMY

from two Greek roots, arrangement/of skin

The art of preparing and preserving the skins of animals, stuffing and mounting
them so as to present the appearance, attitude, etc., of the living animal—O.E.D.

This young man can't get a second date.
His fingers reek of formaldehyde and ammonia,
he's been stuffing birds he snared in Harvard Yard.
Young women find him obsessed
with feathers, beaks, and beady eyes.

A few years later, he's hunting grizzlies
on his ranch. He prefers the Dakota Territory
to the old family brownstone on 20th Street
or the new house on 57th Street.
He's gone out west to strategize.
He needs to rebuild his political career,
he's made too many enemies in New York.

But forget self-preservation,
this is about preservation, taxidermy
and his boyhood home. The family brownstone
becomes a shop. The neighborhood changes,
although his uncle's brownstone stands next door.

Our main character doesn't notice—he's busy,
he's assistant secretary of the Navy,
he's governor, he's nominated for vice-president,
he wins, he succeeds an assassinated president.
He busts trusts, wins the Nobel Prize for peace,
writes half a dozen books, explores Brazil,
gets the River of Doubt renamed for himself,
Rio Teodoro, river of Theodore Roosevelt.
"The only person who makes no mistakes," he says,
"is the person who never does anything."

Now the real story, about the mistake.
After he dies in 1919, the women of his family
raze the shop to rebuild his boyhood home—
boyhood being about motherhood, preservation
being women's work. Rich women's work, mostly.
And for these rich women, it is a religion.

They recreate the nursery, the gym,
his mother's bedroom with her heavy satinwood bed,
the parlor with horsehair chairs and sofas.

They cram the house with bobcat, antelope, deer—
old taxidermy projects. They frame

two smiling wives and six children,
mount old campaign ribbons, dangle pendants
shaped like elephants, new brooms, and a Bull Moose.

"The women did it all," my guide boasts.
"But," I protest, "they broke the rules.
An old building has to be preserved. This is a fake.
The architect copied a demolished building,
then gutted his uncle's house for Teddy's trophies."
"This is the first Victorian reproduction," she says grandly.

I am complaining to an employee
of the Department of the Interior.
If the taxidermist and big game hunter
had not been such a supporter of the Interior,
all this might not have happened.

Pay them a visit at 28 East 20TH Street.
You will imagine young Teddy, upstairs
in his bedroom, stuffing a sparrow,
and cook, down in the basement kitchen,
making a meat-and-potatoes dinner

to run up the dumbwaiter to the family
assembled in the dark dining room
around the mahogany table. They sit uneasily
on chairs with scratchy horsehair seats.
Pretty soon you, too, will feel impatient
to chase bright-feathered birds in Harvard Yard,
or ride out to the Dakota Territory, or paddle
down the River of Doubt which will one day bear your name.

AMERICAN YARD

—live on six networks, December 27, 2000

Next to a Wal-Mart Santa lit-up red,
local police zip body bags.
                        "Three Dead,"
the newsmen count, crowding Field Road to gape
at the small house tied with yellow crime scene tape.
Six cameras pan round the narrow lane
where sound trucks double-park. Producers strain:
"Someone know Jon?"
                             "Know Mills from Guilford High?"
"Good-looking boy."
                         "Not mean, a mixed-up guy."
"He knifed his aunt and cousins," neighbors state.
The chief intones, "Jon Mills, age 28,
sought by police."
                     Anchors line up to show
two brand new scooters that could really go,
two swings twisting without the children's weight.
Raw wind stabs empty seats. Grass fills with snow.

II.

IN A ONE-ROOM HOUSE IN NOVEMBER

Witch hazel opens starry spikes
yellow in leafless, gray-brown woods.
A red-tailed hawk glides through our view,
hunting in snow. Down by the hedge,
the juncos feast on rough wild apples
the color of butter, windfalls on ice.

Two broad blue books compress the world
of words two parted lips invented.
We wonder if a child will speak
our names out loud in this one-room house
where sunlight off the snow swoops up
into the curving, high cove ceiling.

By three the sun's behind the hills,
we know it's late in life and year.
Bare woods attend the day between
trees in bud and trees in leaf
when all the warblers—yellowthroats,
parulas, redstarts—return to sing.

ULTRASOUND PHOTOGRAPH, TWENTY-FOUR WEEKS

Each week she's stronger, kicks me harder,
testing her reach with hands and feet
as I absorb her somersaults
and landings, weightless explorations.

Dreaming of rising suns she stirs.
Wise about dawns, she orbits all
nine planets, chooses one for her
arrival. I swim my laps, she travels

her own slow circles deep within me.
Two fluttering feet, two flexing arms
announce that she's impatient, ready
to run beyond a dark-walled garden.

Her bones glow white as roots beneath
a loamy landscape. Fern-like fists'
curled fingers are unfolding, legs
are springing. August, she'll be blooming.

PREGNANT IN JUNE

The sun-filled tree
kaleidoscopes,
suspends my weight
from small white ropes.

Just breathing makes
the hammock rock.
Eyes close. One wavelet
slaps the dock.

Porch floorboards creak.
A screen door yawns.
Children approach.
On close-mown lawns

wood mallets tap,
croquet balls knock.
That softer sound?
A shuttlecock.

Green apples hang
over my nap.
They'll ripen, drop
in my swaying lap.

STATION ZERO

Progress in childbirth is measured in stations from zero to five.

We've learned a hundred ways to wait. I'm vast,
I breathe in patterns, you count from one to four,
again I breathe, we travel small contractions.
Smiling, you clock each one from start to start.
She's grown so great, we map the county, name
the township, Station Five, where she'll come forth.
You hold me in the landscape of your arms,
you form my ground, low hills, warm soil, white pines.
I am her house, I've shaped her roof and walls
and floor for months, feeling her fill the rooms.
All local weather forms her first bouquet.
I am the house on the hill, the door ajar,
opening slowly. You are meadow, beds
of bright pink clover. Push! She claims this day.

POSTPARTUM PANTOUM

We used the diapers up three days too soon.
She's wet five outfits and the bottom sheet.
I brushed my teeth at one this afternoon.
Our childbirth class was rather incomplete.

She's wet five outfits and the bottom sheet.
I've filled the washer with her little shirts.
Our childbirth class was rather incomplete.
Her toothless smile disarms. Her cry alerts!

I've filled the washer with her little shirts.
Postpartum weeks revolve like a pantoum:
her toothless smile disarms, her cry alerts
triceratops, four bears caged in her room.

Postpartum weeks revolve like a pantoum—
"Oh, won't you take a nap?" we parents croon.
Triceratops, four bears caged in her room
compete with Puddleduck and Mother Loon.

"Oh, won't you take a nap?" we parents croon.
I brushed my teeth at one this afternoon.
Compete with Puddleduck and Mother Loon?
We used the diapers up three days too soon.

NIGHT FEEDING

I.

She's ten days old. Newborn, new mother,
we lock our eyes at feeding time
(human attachment pantomime),
night clocks adjusting to each other.
With one foot kicking, she wakes to dine
at nine for half an hour, eleven,
she calls, again at two, five, seven.
From birth she scents breast milk as mine,
no other mother's. She suckles, slakes
her hunger, lies sated on my shoulder.
I whisper to my mate, "She's fed!"
We croon long songs till sleep overtakes
the three of us. We walk, we hold her,
rub her back. She meets her bed.

2.

We seize the quiet for our own.
Neighbors work late, their headlights touch
and leave us, skin to skin. Bliss, such
soft sounds, wind rises, wind slows down,
live oaks brush tiles on the garden shed.
Under the quilt here hour by hour,
mechanical clocks lose all their power.
We capture night now three abed.
She's six months old. Father and mother,
we lock our eyes at feeding time.
I whisper to him, "Now she's fed,"
so finely tuning to each other,
with infant in this pantomime,
he rubs my back. We love our bed.

LEARNING TO CRAWL

My baby's smiling, lying in her bed.
I know she wants to crawl. Her knees swing wide,
she tucks one arm and rolls onto her side,
extends her other arm and lifts her head.

She pounds her hands, and kicks her feet, and pants
at seven calico stars and a quilted moon.
She's four months old: forward, forward, soon
she wants some forward motion, soon she wants

forward motion. She strains against both hands.
I turn her on her back to rest, but no,
she grins again, and lifts her legs to show
gardens of rosebuds fenced in leafy bands.

She holds her blooming legs up high—count ten!—
then swings her knees and tucks and rolls again.

WEANED

She gobbles handfuls of sand.
Small fingers tease out flies,
deprive the spider, garnish
grass salads and mud pies.

She sinks a fist in my tea
and sucks her warm, sweet hand.
Pillaging trash, she chews
all kinds of contraband.

Grumps Joe, "But this is *girl* stuff.
My two-year-old pulled down
a whole display of chainsaws
at the hardware store in town."

So, gratefully, we plug
the sockets, gate our stair.
She's eating lamb with mint sauce,
mashing green peas in her hair.

VOCABULARY

From her crib at five a.m. she's tossing bears,
rag doll and dormouse over the rail. She hears

my step and calls, "Up! Up!" grasps one more teddy
to start the day with shining eyes, "I ready."

"Hi, Teddy, hi. Hi, Jack. Hi, Biddy-doll,
hi, baby doll. Shirt. Shirt. Skirt. Skirt. A ball."

"Ball, ball. An ap. Ap. Apple, apple. Pear."
"A mouth," she points, "Eyes. Nose. Hair. Mama hair."

She dips a doll's head in her juice. "One, two.
One, two." "Is she drinking, Laura?" "No. Shampoo."

PRIVATE GEOGRAPHY

Laura is standing, walking, climbing up
the five steep steps to Dad who oversees
some grapefruit blooms heavy with bumblebees.
She names the hummingbirds, the ducks, the pup

next door, and learns the words for green and white
and spotted black, for wing and bill and jowl.
She copies as they hover, waddle, growl.
Then, "Why do the coyotes eat at night?"

And "Why are feathers all that's left of Nate?"
(As fast as explanations can be said,
a red-tailed hawk comes gliding overhead.)
Laura—"Oh, Mom!"—next wants me to relate

the wild, the tame, the forager, the fed,
put life and death and baby dolls to bed.

ON THE FAULT LINE

Laurel Canyon, Los Angeles

He loads fresh batteries, type D, three pairs,
into dead flashlights we've ignored for years.
Prepare: earth's plates change gears, groan, scrape, and grind,
dissolve in thirty seconds peace of mind.
We've crowbar, hammer, pet food, leashes, brandy,
plus blankets, camp stove, band-aids, chocolate candy,
some travelers checks (the cash machines might close),
phone lists (long-distance only, we suppose).

So L.A. couples ponder shaking sills:
our safe deposit boxes hold both wills,
our "Quake Awake" alarms (the cost be damned)
give "up to thirty seconds warning" and
our engineer has shown us where to stand,
holding our toddler daughter by the hand.

PLAYING HOUSE

two seven-year olds, overheard

My baby dolls caught colds with a bit of fever.
Let's tuck them into bed with towels for quilts,
let's give them little dolls, they won't get bored.

My Daddy doesn't know it. Mom's a ghost,
but I'm a human female, going to be
his wife when I grow up and we get married.

Here's my favorite doll, Clarisse, she's French.
She's wearing a magenta skirt with dots,
I 'll glue some feathers on her new straw hat.

On the lawn I tossed my Mom's white underwear
and when I turned the sprinkler on—all wet!
You bet, my Mom was mad about my wash!

Let's fly Clarisse to the flowered chair. Let's say,
let's say that it's a garden. Smell the roses!
Today's her birthday, she's turned seventeen.

My Daddy is the one who does the laundry.
He said, "Please pick this up right now, let's find
a better game before it's time for bed."

Clarisse wears braids, should we braid our hair too?
And can we bake some chocolate pudding cake
so she can have her birthday party now?

My Daddy is already married so
I'll have to look for someone else instead.
Girls can propose to anyone they want.

I'd like to make the flowered chair all blue—
a lake. I'll use my left braid for a brush…
it's long enough, tonight I get shampooed.

My Mom is here! She's come to pick me up.
Dear Mom, I need to tell you right away,
I've thought and thought, I'd like to marry…you.

EVERYDAY WARDROBE

When Laura makes a date with older girls,
too bad, they both arrive with Barbie dolls

who bare their breasts and flaunt their wispy weight.
(Those rangy legs would make them 7'8".)

One's hobbled, helpless, but her strut is bold
in toeless, backless five-inch heels of gold,

with red faux fur and matching toque—so fey!—
over a skintight sheath of gold lamé.

The other sports stiff gilt-encrusted lace,
floor-length, with picture hat to frame her face,

her cleavage plummets to the famous waist,
red spike-heel mules confirm her torrid taste.

Poor Laura, scholar's daughter, puzzles, frowns.
"Mommy," she asks, "Where are *your* ball gowns?"

AT SACHEM'S HEAD

Gray-shingled houses speak of summer days
we've spent in boat-filled talk on columned porches,
air sweet with honeysuckle and beach roses,
warm afternoons with just a bit of breeze
to move the little fleet a little faster,
our children sailing in wide, wobbling circles,
learning to ride a stretch of sun-struck water.
Here, I'm a listener, not a talker, sitting
rocking on wooden boards, the wicker creaking,
the loudest sound a motor's tumbling buzz.

FACTS OF LIFE

Two pre-teens disappear
while chicken dinner's cooking.
We parents overhear
nothing. No counting, looking

(that's hide and seek), no ball—
slam, bam—thumping the floor.
So I head to the upstairs hall,
knock on the study door.

"Hi, Mom!" "This is a gas!"
Two heads bend over a book.
"Cathouse." "My ass is grass."
"And bunnyfuck—here, look!"

Their fun's quite scholarly,
Leiter's thick tomes of slang,
all history to me.
They thumb through "crack" and "bang."

Half-page for "chase the duck"?
"Oh, this is hot!" "Let's see!"
Ten pages detail "fuck,"
just like the O.E.D.

Last week I read advice
on giving youth life's facts:
speak truth but be concise,
don't focus on the acts.

"This 'bunnyfuck,'" I say,
distastefully, "Wastes joy.
You might make love all day.
And when you're older, boy

and girl, you'll get to choose."
(But skip the cathouse, please,
drugs, goola box, hard booze,
plus all those STD's,

and tacky, strip-tease clothing.)
"So what's a double-ender?"
"Here's your first clue, it's nothing
to do with sex or gender."

Our mood is casual:
"Did you already guess
the old Morse Code for bull-
shit?" "Baker Sierra." "Yes."

We breathe a Jazz-age mime
of bar and gaming den,
back alleyways of rhyme
replay romance from when

tart slang pursed lips, returned
sweet bite. Next round, I pass:
"The bee's on me. Burn
dinner and I go to grass."

III.

TARGET PRACTICE

Crotophaga ani, local names in the West Indies: Long-Tailed Crow, Tick-Bird,
Merle Corbeau, Garrapetéro (Trickster), Black Daw (Black Slut), Black Witch,
Bouts-Tabac, Bilbitin (Cigarette Butt), Juif or Judío (Jew)

Look for Long-Tailed Crow,
drawling *weu-ik, weu-ik.*
Dark as lumpy coal,

Ani picks ticks, flies
flap, glide, flap, glide, flap, glide.
Big-billed, gawky, slow,

Tick-Bird steals from gardens.
Workers stuff straw dummies,
stone her, *Merle Corbeau!*

Market women bustle
broomsticks, shoo her, *Scat,*
Garrapetéro! Go!

Dockers spit, *Bilbitin,*
Bouts-Tabac, va t'on!
Black Daw, Black Witch—yo!

Listen: on these islands,
names peck and pick on
one Black so-and-so,

brand this bird as Jew or
female, curse at slut or
butt when crops don't grow.

Maybe hate's a kind of
weather. Cyclones clock top
speeds here, tin roofs blow,

nothing stops their rain-filled
rush across the humid
archipelago,

nothing checks their ripping
torrents, tearing circles,
counterclockwise flow.

There's no rainbow. Nesting
in low hedges where blue
heaps of eggs just show,

74

Ani's near the church's
pasture, grooming very
skinny cattle, so

busy picking ticks.
Boy blasts flock, *Judío!*
kills a Long-Tailed Crow.

THE MILLINER'S PROPOSALS

You hear of me, as a respectable architectural man-milliner;
and you send for me, that I may tell you the leading fashion.
—John Ruskin's description of architectural practice

I sew straw hats with yellow-feathered finches
nesting on velvet leaves, stitch canvas hats
billowing like triple-masted ships downwind,
glue leather hats with Gothic buttresses
and gargoyles spouting in the autumn rain,

I upholster hats with alligators eyeing
a muddy satin river, coconut palms.
My red enameled hats pack ladders, working
hoses, pumpers, sirens that shriek your name.
I weave some starry fortunetellers' turbans,

craft hats in cloverleaf of mock-concrete,
coil exit ramps that whiz with tiny cars.
I brim baked hats with pepperoni pizza.
Quite late last night, I sculpted a dozen columns
propping some white felt ones on the golden mean.

All day I tease the voters, sell zest for streets.
They call for me, for public space, for process,
I break dance, sing, sew fancy millinery
with them at city hall, in schools, in churches.
We draw, we sculpt, paint sonnets on the subways,

rhyme couplets on the buses, haiku taxis.
No structure that we make is taller than
the trees. I rose to chief designer here
after we put a playground on every block,
after we put a playground on every single head.

SAPPHICS FOR SAINT URSULA

All eleven thousand of Ursula's girls—
virgin martyrs—died for the faith. We're told they
tested well and entered eternal life as
    innocent maidens,

Brides of Christ. The Ursuline School instructs us:
"Girls, be silent. Silent, prepare your souls for
Jesus." Mother whispers the patron's story,
    rosary rattling—

pagan men assault her unarmed flotilla,
but the Blessed Ursula's pilgrims do not
fight, eleven thousand surrender, maidens
    swooning for sainthood.

Tortures fill our prayer books' thin pages. Missals
harvest virgins' gold-leaf lives, silken ribbons
lash their broken bodies to fasting, feast days,
    bleed them ecstatic,

reap them into kingdom come. Ten years old, we
hymn our praise to starving entranced young women,
silent, bored, we pray to the lost armada:
    bind us forever.

FARANDOLE

—line dance from Provence, where the unmarried launch a town fête
dancing from room to room and house to house

If stanza means a room, a poem can be a house,
a complex Latin villa with space for a carouse,
a Roman vaulted chamber, a stopping place in France,
a Portuguese position, a social thing, a stance.
And a stanza is a branch on a juggler's balance pole.
Before she starts her act, she'll whirl the farandole
from room to house to square. She'll jig past gypsy bands,
upstairs, downstairs she'll wind, always holding hands,
then when she spins gilt globes we'll gaze wide-eyed until
she lands all six bright cups as we applaud her skill,
and when the wine is finished, the café chairs are stacked,
a young man sweeps the street, the juggler's gear is packed.
The farandole is over. Blankets a tangled heap,
back home some brand-new lovers settle down to sleep.

LANGUAGE OF THE FAN

Women are armed with Fans as Men with Swords.
—Addison, *The Spectator*

In corset and bustle, hunting a man,
she who would signal, mastered the fan.

Twirl in left hand, open to view:
"I wish to rid myself of you."

But twirl in right: "I love another."
(You haven't guessed? Your eldest brother.)

Carry the fan in the left hand:
"I'd like to meet you, here I stand..."

Draw through the hand, wear long white gloves:
"I'm hurt, I flaunt my other loves."

Carry the fan in the right hand:
"You seem too willing. I'll command."

Carry the fan in front of face:
"Follow me now! I want a chase!"

Close fan: "I wish to speak to you.
We need a secret rendezvous."

Retreat, advance, no hand's bestowed
until wrists gesture, eyes decode.

Draw fan across the cheek, whisk skirt:
"Of course I love you, though I flirt."

Touch fan to brow when the music halts:
"We're watched! I'll risk just one more waltz!"

ON E-MAIL

You've sent me seven E-mails, abrupt and lean.
Those characters you typed, the bunched-up bytes
you beamed through foreign skies by satellites,
slid through five time zones, entered my laptop screen.

Log on and scan. Punch "quit." Log out. Let's write
letters on sheets that nestle two by two
in light-weight envelopes striped red and blue,
stamped with crowned heads, macaws, date palms, first flight.

Support heart's argument with evidence—
remind me of your touch with tender scrawl,
add salutations and closings, help me recall
romance defies geography and sense.

Punch "save." Download my sonnet, let's refine
love's lettered conversation, way off-line.

CONNOISSEUR

We start this acquaintance
over two mangoes.
You are going to cut them up for dessert,
do the trick
your lover taught you,
make a grid
of flesh extended
from the skin.

I am supposed to be learning
but I don't pay attention,
then you get all my attention:
"Look, it wants to grow."
"Look, this is beautiful."
A green stem is arching out,
tearing from the pit,
breaking its compression. I am interested.

You tell me how to find the next one,
slip in with the big knife,
know the pit is not round but flat.
I must score the skin first,
enter the flesh sideways,
the mass of it and the secret tension.

Keeping the point away from the shoot,
I find it opens perfectly.
I put red grapes on the interstices,
decorate mango flesh
on a blue plate. I hold
another pink and green seed,
exploding,
admired.
But you didn't save it,
I saw you throw them both away.

YESTERDAY I LEARNED THE EARTH IS FLAT

I was never convinced the world
had edges or corners until that plane
drew him out of my day, back
to his city, and I felt old

schedules envelop him, distant
conference rooms wrap his decisions
in travertine and mahogany, felt
his family reclaim him, pleased

to see him unpack, eat dinner,
praise his son's baseball team,
and his wife's *coq au vin*.
Printed on me he left signs

of sudden light, direct positives,
his breath on my cheek, a kiss
on my shoulder when he wanted
to wake me. Tonight I'll quiz

dead cartographers, scour imagined
corners, add my name to lost explorers
who insisted earth must hold
one more continent—and sailed off.

CADILLAC RANCH, 1999

—ten classic Cadillacs, 1949–1963, designed by Harley Earl in the era of
"dynamic obsolescence," placed in a Texas field by Ant Farm, 1974

I cruise those years nose-down in Texas sand
and count ten styles of iridescent fins.
The gum ball Amarillo sun begins
to sink in smog, time's yellow reprimand—
chrome rusts, paint flakes, rolled steel endures, ten low,
wide bodies languish reddish-brownish-black.
Sleek shapes sit stouter, softer. Almost slack.
Glove leather desiccates. Graffiti now—
fuck you, fuck, fuck—slipcovers back seat space.
Rear windshields, crazed, punched-out and gaping raw,
mock mid-life crises, missing teeth, the law.
There's still some provocation in the place.
Ten miles a gallon. New car every year.
Aging bodies warn us: learn to steer.

LUNCH WITH GIAMBATTISTA NOLLI

Architect and surveyor of *Pianta Grande di Roma*, the first modern city map, 1748.
"Despite praise heaped on the work by everyone from the pope on down, it was not
a financial success.... After two years, most engraved copies were still unsold."

Remember when we two young architects
recorded a street with a dozen crooked houses?
I draw all Rome now, every way-out quarter,
the Pope himself signed me a pass, I measure
everything—yes, even cloistered convents.
Rolling and clanking my iron chain, I slice
at space, cut ground and figure, figure and ground.
The riverbanks and cypresses, you'll know,
the plan is new, stretched flat on twelve wide sheets.

"Lacks charm," a colleague carps, blind to the grid
as science. "No taste, no style," a rival sneers.
"Buy it," the barefoot friars beg their abbots.
They swear the saints themselves guide my *bussola!*

No one has ever drawn a map like mine,
or understood its mathematic power,
or counted up its thousand uses—taxing,
policing, buying, selling, spying, wooing—
that's not to mention ordinary viewing.

You build, my friend, you know our art is urban.
Just four *zecchini*. No? I wager you—
some day we'll all own city maps in Rome.
So please, be one of the first, put down your cash!

GOOD OLD DEMOCRACY

Grand Anse, Grenada

DECEMBER 20, 2000, 9:00 A.M.

Yawning with jet lag, slung in a canvas chair
under a sea-grape tree, I scribble cards.
Beach peddlers tease my nose with cloves and bay,

with cinnamon and nutmegs tipped with mace
looped on long kitchen necklaces for stoves.
Women shake out batiks from shabby totes:

"Just thirty-five U.S.—a pareo?"
"Beach dress, a lovely red with stars for you?"
"Small one in blue for your young missy? *Guapa!*"

One waves a comb, glass beads, and crumpled foil,
"Some cornrows? Braid long hair for little miss?"
"So sorry, no." "Tomorrow, then?" "We'll see."

DECEMBER 21, 6 P.M.

"I vote for G.O.D.," our waitress says.
I nod, "Is that some kind of Christian party?"
"Good Old Democracy." Her boyfriend laughs,

"Hopeless! The G.O.D., they give some jobs,
they give some land, but they want public hangings!"
Bananaquits ravage stray crusts of bread.

The pool boy teaches me to strip a frond
of palm right back to the stalk, to tie a noose
and lead a bright green lizard on a leash.

Bats snatch mosquitoes in the evening air.
"Beach dress? Some braids? Six dollars, I make three?"
"No, thank you." "Well, tomorrow then?" "We'll see."

DECEMBER 22, 1 P.M.

At a beachfront house with clapboards painted purple,
radio pounds, "I'm goin' with him, my Jesus!"
We taste plantains, fried kingfish, callalloo

washed down with cold rum punch. Replete and sleepy,
we scan a carnival of wooden skiffs,
teal blue with bands of green and tangerine,

lemon striped violet and pink. Old motors
sputter, drag skiers through the brilliant sea.
Small boys take turns to surf on an old door,

giggle, "Who next? Who next?" "One more!" "One more!"
She's back. "I braid your hair with little beads?"
"Beach dress?" "No, we are leaving now," I say.

DECEMBER 24, 3 P.M.

Languor of tulip, genip, traveler's palm,
of long black pods moored fast on ferny lace—
ylang-ylang and nutmeg scent the air,

crushed nutmegs pave the way to cottage beds.
Rain pounds long grooves of corrugated tin,
we rise to double rainbows, cloud-wreathed peaks.

Stray kittens, sheltered underneath our porch,
emerge, scrawny and scared, mewing for milk.
It's ordinary enough—unless starvation

is blooming here. It's not indigenous.
"A pareo? I do your hair in cornrows?"
The peddler found us! "Not right now," I say.

DECEMBER 25, NOON

Sidewheels churn foam, the flatboat band blares carols,
glides to a sheltered, silent, unspoiled bay
brilliant with bougainvillea. And down they run,

down from the ridge, a hundred peddlers run,
bearing their homemade necklaces of nutmegs
and shells, their spices, plastic combs, and cloth.

Wares high, the hawkers crowd. We bump the pier.
"You'll want some things *today*, I know," she says,
"some things for Christmas Day." Old triangles

of trade and war explode from her black tote.
I point to stars, she folds the galaxy,
sells me red stars to wrap wet bathing suits.

ON THE HUNDRED-PERCENT CORNER

*Academic couples improve their chances in a tight job market
if they are willing to try a long-distance commute.*

On the plane, I'm talking tough, like a pioneer.
I plat a town with the string, the stakes, the tents,
name unpaved streets Equality and Progress.

He wrestles a Conestoga. Oxen balk
and hex signs blaze like prairie stars. He steers
around old ruts, veers off the trail, heads back

on the inside curve of a creek he'll have to ford,
later. But watch, he'll raft that painted wagon,
provision us in Independence, push on.

I fly today, barter a Boston evening
for a sere late California afternoon,
charged to our joint account. Below me spin

alfalfa circles, green as the all-seeing eye
on the dollar. *Annuit coeptis:* God
Smiles on Our Undertakings. I am aware

grit desert shifts beneath those leafy clocks.
Look down: commercial blocks, wide open sky,
Loving, Utopia, and Roaring Springs.

Dry crossroads yawn at nowhere: Earth and Spur
and Matador, Happy, Goodnight, and Muleshoe,
risk-takers' towns we might have passed through then.

We claim both work and love. Our trail winds on,
arched like an oxbow, pioneers' old crosses
nailed and named, every mazy mile.

NOTES

FOR RENT Mount Olympus—tract in the Laurel Canyon area of Los Angeles. Skywriting—a typical word is three and a half miles long.

INVITATION TO MR. JOHN BRINCKERHOFF JACKSON J.B. Jackson (1909–1996), essayist and cultural geographer, founder of *Landscape* magazine, opened Harvard students' eyes to modest frame houses, yards, and roadside buildings. I borrowed the form from Elizabeth Bishop's "An Invitation to Miss Marianne Moore," which Bishop in turn had borrowed from Pablo Neruda's "Alberto Rojas Jimenez vienes volando."

SECOND MARRIAGE After a forest fire, new growth emerges from seeds that sprout during extreme heat.

REVENGE WITH ICE PALACE All of the construction details are correct. Fantastic buildings made for winter carnivals often reached ten stories high.

NOLLI *Bussola*—magnetic compass. *Zecchini*—coin.

GOOD OLD DEMOCRACY Grenada is a former British colony in the West Indies. Grenadans elected Maurice Bishop as president. He led a popular revolution emphasizing literacy, equality, and jobs. (Red stars were part of the logo.) The United States refused economic aid. A far-left group assassinated Bishop in 1983. U.S. Marines invaded to support a right-wing strongman. The economy has not recovered. Good Old Democracy (G.O.D.) is one of several active political parties today. *Guapa*—pretty.

ON THE HUNDRED-PERCENT CORNER Hundred-percent corner—1920s real estate slang for the site of greatest retail opportunity, where main streets cross and people meet. Independence, Missouri—start of the Overland Trail. Loving, Goodnight, Happy, Roaring Springs, Utopia, and Muleshoe are the names of real towns in Texas.

DOLORES HAYDEN

Dolores Hayden is an urban historian and architect whose poems have appeared in *The Kenyon Review, The Yale Review, Southwest Review, Michigan Quarterly Review, Crab Orchard Review, Witness, Poetry Northwest, Slate,* and *Verse Daily.* She has won the Poetry Society of America's *The Writer Magazine*/Emily Dickinson Award. A former Guggenheim and N.E.A. fellow, she is also the author of several award-winning books about American cities, including *The Power of Place* (The M.I.T. Press, 1995) and *Building Suburbia* (Pantheon, 2003). Her most recent non-fiction book is *A Field Guide to Sprawl* (W.W. Norton, 2004). She is a professor of architecture and American studies at Yale University.

Breinigsville, PA USA
02 January 2010
252482BV00001B/49/A